THE
MAGNIFICENT
BOOK
❖ OF ❖
ANIMALS

THE MAGNIFICENT BOOK OF ANIMALS

ILLUSTRATED BY
Val Walerczuk

WRITTEN BY
Tom Jackson

Silver Dolphin

Silver Dolphin Books
An imprint of Printers Row Publishing Group
A division of Readerlink Distribution Services, LLC
10350 Barnes Canyon Road, Suite 100, San Diego, CA 92121
www.silverdolphinbooks.com

Produced by Weldon Owen Children's Books
An imprint of Weldon Owen International LP.
PO Box 3088
San Rafael, CA 94912
www.insighteditions.com

Printers Row Publishing Group is a division of Readerlink Distribution Services, LLC.
Silver Dolphin Books is a registered trademark of Readerlink Distribution Services, LLC.

All notations of errors or omissions should be addressed to Silver Dolphin Books,
Editorial Department, at the above address.

The Library of Congress has cataloged the original Silver Dolphin edition as follows:

Names: Walerczuk, Val, illustrator. | Jackson, Tom, 1972- , author.
Title: The magnificent book of animals / illustrated by Val Walerczuk; written by Tom Jackson.
Description: San Diego, California : Silver Dolphin Books, 2017.
Identifiers: LCCN 2016020956 | ISBN 9781626867420
Subjects: LCSH: Mammals. | Mammals--Pictorial works.
Classification: LCC QL706 .W15 2017 | DDC 599--dc23
LC record available at https://lccn.loc.gov/2016020956

ISBN: 978-1-64517-102-7
Manufactured, printed, and assembled in Humen, China.
First printing, August 2019. RRD/08/19
23 22 21 20 19 1 2 3 4 5

Introduction

From the icy Arctic to the hot African savanna, animals live in every corner of the world. They can be found swinging from trees, snuggling underground, or scaling the tallest mountain peaks. And some of the largest, most amazing creatures on Earth are mammals.

Mammals are warm-blooded, give birth to live offspring, feed milk to their young, and are covered in hair. This may sound familiar—humans are mammals, too! In fact, there are more than 5,000 different types of mammals living all over the world. They can be cute and cuddly, smart and stealthy, or fierce and ferocious.

The Magnificent Book of Animals showcases some of the most fascinating mammals on the planet through oversized, stunning illustrations. Amazing facts accompany every animal, describing the behavior that makes each one unique. The illustrations and fascinating facts bring the animals to life and provide a sneak peek into what you could expect if you came into contact with these animals in the wild.

Fact file

Lives: North America

Habitat: Mountain forest

Length: 5.5–9 feet

Weight: 290–790 pounds

Life span: 25–30 years

Diet: Fish, deer, and fruits

Learn about the playful chimpanzee, the sleepy koala, the lumbering hippopotamus, and more magnificent animals inside!

Contents

African elephant

- An African elephant's tusks are its two front teeth. They can be as long as an adult human.

- A baby African elephant eats a little of its mother's poop. The bacteria help to keep its stomach healthy!

- African elephants communicate with each other using deep rumbles that travel through the ground as vibrations.

- African elephants are Earth's biggest land mammals.

- An African elephant's trunk has more than 100,000 different muscles.

Fact file

Lives: Africa

Habitat: Forests and grasslands

Height: 10–13 feet

Weight: 3,750–13,450 pounds

Life span: 60–70 years

Diet: Roots, leaves, grasses, fruit, and bark

An African elephant's teeth are so huge that there is only room for four teeth at a time in its mouth. It grows new ones as each tooth gradually wears down and falls out.

 An African elephant's wrinkly skin traps droplets of moisture, which helps to keep it cool in the hot sun.

Giant panda

- The giant panda has a sixth "finger" on each forepaw, where a wrist bone sticks out to hold bamboo shoots, their favorite food.

- A panda has to eat constantly. It can sleep for only four hours at a time before it has to wake up to eat some more.

- Pandas peel off the outside of the bamboo with their teeth and then eat the softer insides.

- Giant pandas like to be alone. If two pandas meet, they will usually growl and hit each other until one runs away.

- A panda poops 40 times a day!

- Male pandas do handstands so that they can use glands on their rear ends to leave scent marks on tree trunks.

- Newborn panda cubs are 900 times smaller than a female adult. That makes them the smallest babies of any mammal apart from marsupials.

Fact file

Lives: China

Habitat: Bamboo forest

Length: 4–6 feet

Weight: 220–330 pounds

Life span: 15–20 years

Diet: Bamboo

Reindeer

 True reindeer live in Europe and Asia. Their very close cousins, called caribou, live in North America.

 Male reindeer are called bulls, while females are called cows.

Reindeer are the only type of deer where both males and females grow antlers.

Reindeer are very strong swimmers.

 Reindeer are the only mammals that can see ultraviolet light, which has rays so short most humans cannot see it.

In winter, when the tundra is covered in snow, a reindeer eats only bark, twigs, and its favorite food, lichen.

In summer, reindeer have short brown coats; in winter their coats are gray and much shaggier.

A male reindeer has antlers in summer; a female has antlers during the winter.

Fact file

Lives: Arctic region

Habitat: Tundra and forests

Length: 5–7.5 feet

Weight: 130–700 pounds

Life span: 10–15 years

Diet: Leaves, grass, twigs, mushrooms, and lichen

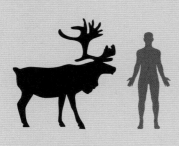

Gray wolf

- A group of wolves is called a pack. The pack works together to hunt down large animals as prey.

- Gray wolves used to live all over North America, but today they are mostly found in Alaska, Michigan, Wisconsin, Montana, Idaho, Oregon, and Wyoming.

- A wolf cub's eyes are blue, but as it gets older they turn yellow.

- The howl of a wolf can be heard up to ten miles away.

- All domestic dogs have descended from tame wolves that started to live alongside people about 20,000 years ago.

Fact file

Lives: North America, Asia, eastern and northern Europe

Habitat: Tundra and forest

Length: 5 feet

Weight: 180–200 pounds

Life span: 8–13 years

Diet: Rabbits, deer, and rodents

A wolf can eat 20 pounds of food in one meal. That's equivalent to a human eating 100 hamburgers.

Despite all the myths and legends, wolves rarely attack humans.

Mandrill

- The mandrill is the largest monkey in the world. The males are too big to climb high into trees.

- A male mandrill's lips are often stuck in a snarl so it shows off its long teeth.

- When a male mandrill is angry, the colors on his face become brighter and he thumps the ground with his hands.

- Mandrills live in huge groups called hordes. The largest horde ever counted contained 1,200 mandrills.

Fact file

Lives: Central Africa

Habitat: Lowland forest

Length: 2.5–3 feet

Weight: 22–77 pounds

Life span: 20–30 years

Diet: Fruit, nuts, roots, and small animals

Mandrills save food for later by stuffing it into pouches in their cheeks.

 In addition to a blue-and-red face and pale yellow beard, male mandrills have a purple bottom.

17

Flying fox

- Flying foxes are the largest fruit bats in the world. They are ten times bigger than the smallest bat species.

- The wingspan of a flying fox can be up to five feet across.

- Flying foxes eat fruit and flowers. They hang from trees and grab food with claws on their wings.

- Flying foxes find food using their large eyes and sensitive noses.

- Bats sleep upside down in caves and trees.

- When they are thirsty, flying foxes swoop low over water and then fly back to the roost to lick the water off their belly fur.

- A bat's wings are made of skin stretched between its very long finger bones.

Fact file

Lives: Southeast Asia, Australia

Habitat: Rain forest

Length: 7–9 inches

Weight: 1 pound 4 ounces–
2 pounds 6 ounces

Life span: 15 years

Diet: Flowers and fruit

Snow leopard

- Most big cats—like lions and tigers—can roar, but snow leopards cannot.

- The snow leopard holds the animal long jump record. It can leap 49 feet—that's longer than a school bus!

- The snow leopard wraps its bushy tail around its feet to keep warm while resting in the snow.

- The snow leopard's smoky gray camouflage hides it so well in snowy terrain that it is known as the "ghost cat."

- This cat can climb two-thirds of the way up Mount Everest, making it the highest-hunting mammal in the world.

- The snow leopard's spots become paler in winter so it can hide better among the snow-covered rocks.

- A mother snow leopard lines her den with her own shed fur to make it warm for her cubs.

Fact file

Lives: Central Asia

Habitat: Mountains

Length: 3–4 feet

Weight: 75–120 pounds

Life span: 9–10 years

Diet: Sheep, goats, deer, and smaller mammals such as marmots

Przewalski's horse

- Przewalski's horses are the oldest breed of horse alive today.

- These horses are named after the Russian explorer Nikolai Przewalski. He brought them to the attention of scientists in the late 1800s.

- Przewalski's horses were first discovered in Mongolia, a remote country in Asia.

- Most Przewalski's horses alive today live in zoos, but their ancestors were never domesticated or kept as livestock.

- All horses' eyes are positioned on either side of their heads. They can look at things around them, but cannot see what is directly in front of them.

Fact file

Lives: Worldwide today, but originally China, Mongolia, and parts of Russia and Europe.

Habitat: Grasslands, semidesert

Height: 4–4.5 feet

Weight: 440–750 pounds

Life span: 20 years

Diet: Grass and leaves

Horses can smell water from many miles away.

 A herd of horses is led by one large male, called the stallion. The rest of the herd are females, called mares.

Red kangaroo

Fact file

Lives: Australia
Habitat: Grassland
Height: 32–64 inches
Weight: 44–180 pounds
Life span: 6–8 years
Diet: Grass and shrubs

- A female kangaroo is called a jill; a male is known as a jack; a baby is a joey.
- The red kangaroo is the largest marsupial still alive today.
- A newborn joey weighs just 0.04 ounces and crawls through its mother's fur to her pouch.
- The red kangaroo can jump as far as 25 feet at one time.
- When standing still, the kangaroo uses its thick tail for balance.
- A kangaroo fights like a boxer, jumping forward and punching its attacker with its front paws.
- A joey stays in its mother's pouch for at least six months before it is strong enough to start exploring outside.

Lion

- Lions are the only cats that live in family groups.

- These family groups are called prides. They can include as many as 40 lions. Most of those are female, and three or fewer are male.

- A lion's mane tells how old the animal is. Older lions have darker manes.

- A lion's stomach stretches so that it can eat a quarter of its body weight in one meal.

Fact file

Lives: Africa (and the Gir Forest in India)

Habitat: Grassland

Length: 5–6.5 feet

Weight: 265–550 pounds

Life span: 10–14 years

Diet: Antelopes and zebras

Lions are the only cats to have a tassel on their tails. They raise the tassel to show where they are in tall grass.

 A lion's tongue is very rough. This helps the lion to lick the meat off of bones.

 The male lions in a pride rarely hunt—the female lionesses do it for him. However, he gets to eat first.

 A lion's roar can be heard from four or five miles away.

Polar bear

- A polar bear's hairs are not white—they are transparent. Light reflecting off of them makes them look white.

- Polar bears have black skin, which soaks up the sun's heat and helps to keep them warm.

- These animals spend the summer at sea, walking on the frozen ocean or swimming up to 60 miles to find food.

- Polar bears do not sleep or hibernate. However, pregnant females dig a den into the snow and live off of their fat reserves during their pregnancy.

- Cubs are born inside the winter snow den, usually in late January.

Fact file

Lives: The Arctic

Habitat: Ice and tundra

Length: 6.5–8 feet

Weight: 330–1,100 pounds

Life span: 15–18 years

Diet: Seals, fish, deer, and berries

Polar bears have four inches of fat under their skin. This keeps them warm and acts as a food store for when they cannot hunt.

 Polar bears feed on seals. They can smell their prey through the ice that covers the ocean.

Dromedary

🐪 Dromedaries are sometimes called Arabian camels, and they have one hump. Bactrian camels from Asia have two humps.

🐪 A dromedary's hump stores fat, not water, but the animal's body can break down the fat into water and energy. This helps to keep the camel alive as it walks across deserts where little food is found.

🐪 A dromedary can go for months without eating.

🐪 A dromedary closes its nostrils to prevent it from inhaling sand during a sandstorm.

Fact file

Lives: Africa, Middle East

Habitat: Desert

Length: 10 feet

Weight: 660–1,520 pounds

Life span: 40–50 years

Diet: Plants

When frightened, camels may spit some of their stomach juices at the threat.

A baby dromedary has no hump, just a tassel of hairs where one will grow later.

Orangutan

- Baby orangutans live with their mothers for up to seven years, which is longer than any other wild animal.

- Orangutans have been observed using large leaves as umbrellas.

- An orangutan's arms are much longer than its legs. When an orangutan stands up, its arms almost touch the ground.

- Orangutans eat at least 300 different types of fruit as well as leaves, insects, flowers, eggs, and tree bark.

- Orangutans are the largest tree-dwelling mammals on Earth. Unlike other great apes, they spend the majority of their lives high in the treetops.

Fact file

Lives: Sumatra and Borneo

Habitat: Rain forest

Length: 4–5 feet

Weight: 66–200 pounds

Life span: 35–45 years

Diet: Fruits, leaves, and eggs

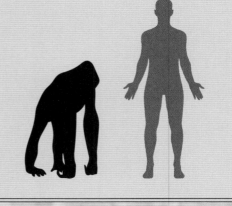

Orangutans build a fresh nest each night out of leafy branches so they can sleep high in the trees.

Orangutan means "person of the forest" in the Malay language.

Okapi

An okapi's tongue is so long that it can lick its eyes and ears clean.

Okapi calves keep track of their mothers in dense forest by looking for the stripes on her rump.

An okapi can listen to two sounds at once by twisting its ears to point in different directions.

Only the male okapi has horns. They point backward so they do not get tangled in tree branches.

Scent glands on an okapi's hooves produce a sticky substance that leaves a trail of scent wherever it goes.

Fact file

Lives: Central Africa

Habitat: Rain forest

Length: 6–8 feet

Weight: 45–770 pounds

Life span: 20–30 years

Diet: Leaves, twigs, and fruit

Okapis communicate with sounds so low that predators (and humans) cannot hear them.

 The stripes and red-brown coat of an okapi makes these animals very difficult to see among the tree trunks and branches of the shady forest.

Grizzly bear

🐻 Grizzly bears are a type of brown bear that live mostly in the northern United States, Alaska, and Canada.

🐻 As grizzlies get older, their fur develops whitish, or grizzled, tips. That's how they got their name.

🐻 Newborn grizzly bear cubs hum as they drink their mother's milk.

🐻 Grizzlies have a hump between their shoulders. This contains the huge muscles that control their front legs.

🐻 Grizzly bears cover their leftover food with moss and grass. Chemicals in the moss keep the food from rotting.

Fact file

Lives: North America

Habitat: Mountain forest

Length: 5.5–9 feet

Weight: 290–790 pounds

Life span: 25–30 years

Diet: Fish, deer, and fruits

Grizzly bears can lose a third of their weight as they hibernate, or sleep, through the winter.

 During hibernation, grizzlies don't eat or go to the bathroom at all. This can last as long as six months.

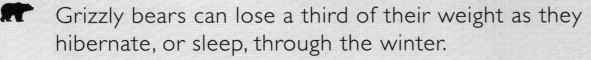

Chimpanzee

Fact file

Lives: Central Africa

Habitat: Tropical rain forest

Length: 4–5 feet

Weight: 70–130 pounds

Life span: 45 years

Diet: Plants, insects, and small mammals

🐾 Chimpanzees are more closely related to humans than any other animal.

🐾 Young chimpanzees can live with their mothers for as long as ten years.

🐾 Chimps communicate with facial expressions. A big grin means a chimp is scared, not happy.

🐾 Chimps chew the ends of sticks and then use them like sponges to soak up water. They also use rocks to break open nuts to eat.

🐾 Chimps make friends by kissing each other and grooming bugs out of each other's fur.

🐾 Like humans, chimps have thumbs that allow them to hold onto things like food or tree branches.

Unlike other apes, chimps work as a team to hunt for prey, such as monkeys and small deer.

39

Arctic fox

The Arctic fox's coat changes color. In winter it is white; in summer it turns gray-brown. This helps the animals blend into their surroundings.

During winter blizzards, Arctic foxes sometimes tunnel into the snow to keep themselves warm.

The Arctic fox has small ears compared to other foxes, but it has excellent hearing. In fact, it can hear lemmings, its favorite food, scurrying around under deep snow.

Arctic foxes can withstand a temperature of -58°F. Any colder than that, and it stays in its den until it warms up.

Fact file

Lives: The Arctic

Habitat: Tundra

Length: 31–50 inches, including its tail

Weight: 6.5–20 pounds

Life span: 3–6 years

Diet: Rabbits, voles, lemmings, fish, berries, and mushrooms

The Arctic fox is the only land mammal native to Iceland.

If it cannot find its own food, an Arctic fox will follow a polar bear and eat its leftovers.

Tapir

- Tapirs look a little like pigs, but horses and rhinos are their closest relatives.

- The tapir's body is narrow at the front and wide at the back, which helps it to push through thick undergrowth.

- Their trunklike noses are flexible and can wrap around branches to strip off leaves.

- The Malayan tapir's black-and-white body helps it to hide among patches of moonlight and shadow in the forest.

- Tapirs hide in the water when they feel threatened. They go under completely, leaving only their noses above the surface so they can breathe.

Fact file

Lives: Southeast Asia, Mexico, South America, and Central America

Habitat: Forests and swamps

Length: 5.5–8.5 feet

Weight: 550–830 pounds

Life span: 30 years

Diet: Leaves, fruits, and berries

Tapirs are most active during the twilight hours of dawn and dusk, and usually sleep during the day.

 Tapirs whistle to each other through the dense undergrowth of their forest habitat.

Tiger

- Tigers mark their territory by scraping claw marks into trees and rocks.

- Unlike most cats, tigers like water. They swim across rivers and lie in wait for prey in the shallow water.

- A tiger kills one or two animals each week. It buries the leftovers to eat later.

- Tigers are such powerful hunters that they can kill animals that weigh four times more than they do.

Fact file

Lives: Southern and eastern Asia
Habitat: Forests and swamps
Length: 6.5–10.5 feet
Weight: 145–675 pounds
Life span: 10–12 years
Diet: Deer, cattle, and pigs

Baby tigers begin hunting with their mothers when they are about two months old.

 Tigers are the world's largest wild cats.

 A tiger controls a huge territory—females need an average of 8 square miles, while males may control up to 40 square miles.

Warthog

- Warthogs enter their burrows backward so they can be ready to defend themselves against intruders.

- When warthogs are running from danger, they raise their tails to warn others.

- The warts on a warthog's face are there to protect its eyes during fights.

- Warthogs are related to pigs. They use their piglike snouts to sniff out buried food.

- Warthogs kneel down to get closer to the ground when they are eating grass.

Fact file

Lives: Africa

Habitat: Grassland and woodland

Length: 3–5 feet

Weight: 110–330 pounds

Life span: 12–15 years

Diet: Grass, roots, and berries

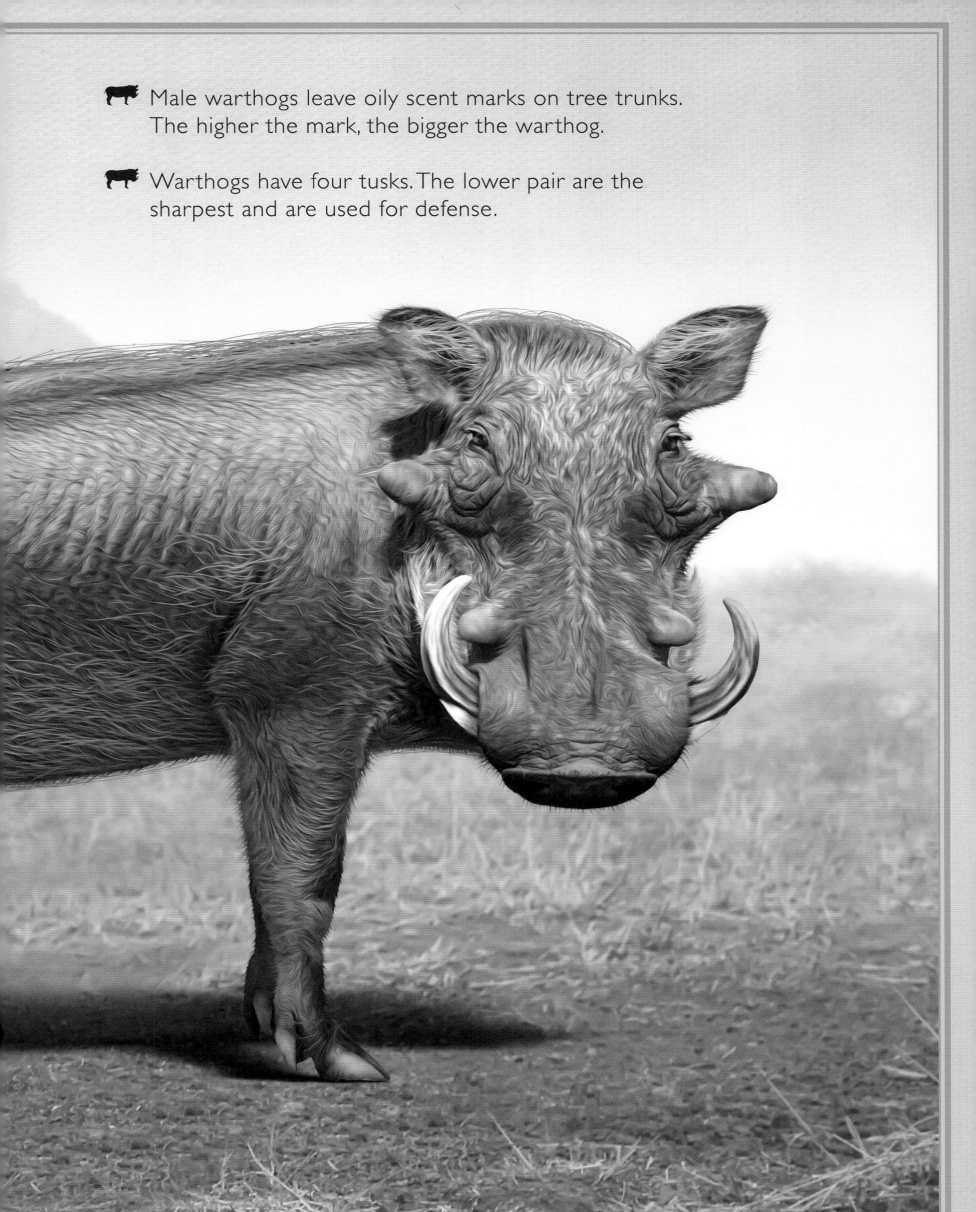

Male warthogs leave oily scent marks on tree trunks. The higher the mark, the bigger the warthog.

Warthogs have four tusks. The lower pair are the sharpest and are used for defense.

Beaver

- A beaver's front teeth never stop growing. They are worn down by chewing wood.

- A beaver can cover its eyes with clear eyelids. These work like goggles and help the beaver to see underwater.

- Beavers dam rivers with mud and logs to make the water much deeper. This protects them against predators, and enables them to keep food and building materials afloat.

- Beavers build homes called lodges by making a pile of mud, wood, and stones and then burrowing out a den.

- The outside of their muddy lodge freezes solid in winter, making it impossible for predators to dig into it.

Fact file

Lives: Europe, Asia, and North America

Habitat: Rivers and lakes

Length: 30–50 inches, including tail

Weight: 25–65 pounds

Life span: 24 years

Diet: Grasses and wood pulp

Inside, the lodge has two rooms. The entrance chamber is used for drying off, and the inner den is kept dry for sleeping.

Beavers use their paddlelike tails for steering in water.

Giraffe

🦒 The giraffe is the tallest animal in the world. It can be more than 15 feet tall.

🦒 Giraffes have seven neck bones—the same number as a human being.

🦒 The tongue of a giraffe is a dark bluish-purple. It is 20 inches long and is very flexible.

🦒 Male giraffes fight by knocking their necks together.

🦒 Giraffes have one of the shortest sleep requirements of any mammal. They sleep only ten minutes to two hours per day.

🦒 A giraffe is born with two hair-covered horns called ossicones. They are flat on the head at birth but grow longer as the giraffe gets older.

Female giraffes give birth standing up. The baby falls six feet to the ground.

A giraffe's heart beats twice as hard and twice as fast as a human's to pump blood up the animal's long neck to reach its head.

Fact file

Lives: Africa

Habitat: Woodland and savanna

Length: 12.5–15.5 feet

Weight: 1,500–3,000 pounds

Life span: 25 years

Diet: Leaves

Koala

- Koalas sleep for 20 hours each day.

- Koalas are marsupials, a type of animal whose mothers carry their babies in a pouch on their bellies.

- Koalas keep their fur clean by combing it with a long claw on their front paws.

- Koalas smell of eucalyptus, which comes from the oily eucalyptus leaves that they eat.

- Fossils show that 100,000 years ago, there was a type of koala that was the size of a cow.

- A koala's small brain floats in fluid, which cushions it if the koala falls out of a tree and lands on its head.

- Every now and then, a koala will eat a mouthful of soil. The germs in the soil help it to digest leaves.

Fact file

Lives: Eastern Australia

Habitat: Woodlands and forests

Length: 2–2.5 feet

Weight: 9–33 pounds

Life span: 13–18 years

Diet: Eucalyptus leaves

Zebra

 Zebras sleep standing up.

 Every zebra has a unique pattern of black (or brown) stripes on white fur.

🐎 Zebras have black skin. Black and white hairs make up their stripes.

🐎 Zebra stripes have many uses, including repelling biting flies, keeping the animals cool, and offering camouflage.

🐎 The stripes make a herd of zebras blend together so that it's difficult for lions and other predators to follow one target in the crowd.

🐎 Zebra herds are always on the move, following the lead of a chief male, or stallion.

Fact file

Lives: Africa

Habitat: Savanna and mountains

Length: 6.5–8.5 feet

Weight: 500–900 pounds

Life span: 40 years

Diet: Grass

Zebras dig into dry riverbeds with their hooves to make small watering holes.

 Zebras prefer to eat the tender tops of grass blades and leave the thicker stalks behind.

Sloth

🦥 Sloths move very slowly along branches, making it less likely that eagles and other predators will notice them.

🦥 Their long, shaggy fur gets very dirty and turns green from all the mold and algae living in it.

🦥 A sloth can do almost anything it needs to in the trees—except go to the bathroom. It moves to the ground to do that—and only about once a week.

🦥 Sloths have weak muscles, but that makes them light enough to climb out along flimsy branches to reach fresh leaves.

A sloth is born in the trees and must grab its mother's long hair to keep itself from falling to the ground.

Sloths do everything slowly, even digest their food. Sometimes it takes a sloth an entire month to digest one meal.

Fact file

Lives: Central and South America

Habitat: Rain forest

Length: 20–30 inches

Weight: 10–20 pounds

Life span: 20–30 years

Diet: Leaves, stems, and fruit

57

Bison

- During the 19th century, hunters killed at least 50 million bison in North America.

- The American bison is sometimes called a buffalo, but it is only a distant relative of the real buffaloes that live in Africa and Asia.

- Their winter coats are so thick and well insulated that snow can cover their backs without melting.

- In spring, bison shed their thick winter coats.

- Bison have poor eyesight, but they can smell another animal up to two miles away.

Fact file

Lives: North America

Habitat: Woodlands and prairie

Length: 6.5–11.5 feet

Weight: 795–2,200 pounds

Life span: 15–20 years

Diet: Grass

A healthy adult bison has no natural enemies. Predators such as wolves and mountain lions attack only the young and the very old.

Bison are good swimmers. Their bodies float in the water.

Hippopotamus

- The word *hippopotamus* means "river horse" in Greek.

- A hippo's skin produces a red liquid that works like a moisturizer and sunscreen.

- Hippos yawn to show their enemies that they are ready for a fight.

- Hippos stay submerged in water to stay cool during the day. At night they leave the water to eat grass.

- Hippo babies weigh about 100 pounds when they are born.

- A group of hippos is called a school, herd, or bloat.

Fact file

Lives: Africa

Habitat: Rivers and lakes

Length: 10–16 feet

Weight: 3,000–9,000 pounds

Life span: 40 years

Diet: Grass

A hippo's skin is about two and a half inches thick.

 A hippo can close its ears and nostrils when it dives underwater.

Gorilla

The word *gorilla* comes from the ancient Greek term for "tribe of hairy women."

A group of gorillas, called a troop, is led by the dominant male, often called a silverback due to the gray hair on his back.

Gorillas eat a large breakfast of leaves and fruit, and then take a midday nap.

Gorillas scare attackers away by slapping their chests with cupped hands. This makes a loud thumping sound.

A gorilla troop moves to a new place in the forest every day to find fresh food.

Young gorillas spend most of their time playing, much like human children.

Fact file

Lives: Central Africa

Habitat: Lowland tropical forests

Length: 5–5.5 feet

Weight: 300–400 pounds

Life span: 35 years

Diet: Leaves, fruit, roots, and other plants

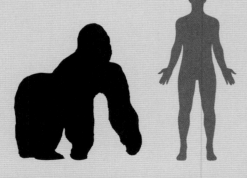

White rhinoceros

 A white rhino's skin is not white but gray-brown.

 The word *rhinoceros* means "nose horn."

 Rhino horns are made from keratin, which is the same material that makes up human hair and fingernails.

 Adult rhinos keep their horns sharp by rubbing them against trees.

 Male rhinos can charge at their enemies at speeds up to 30 mph.

Fact file

Lives: Africa

Habitat: Grassy savanna

Length: 12–14 feet

Weight: 3,000–7,000 pounds

Life span: 50 years

Diet: Grass

A rhino's huge head and horns alone can weigh 1,100 pounds.

 Rhinos may let oxpecker birds ride on their backs. In return, the birds keep the rhinos' skin free of ticks and other parasites.

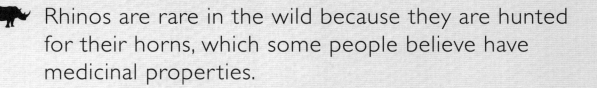 Rhinos are rare in the wild because they are hunted for their horns, which some people believe have medicinal properties.

Wolverine

- Wolverines look like hairy dogs, but they are actually related to weasels.

- Wolverines have wide feet that work like snowshoes so that the animals do not sink in deep snow.

- Wolverines have long claws that they use for climbing and digging.

- Baby wolverines, or kits, are born in winter and have white fur to blend in with the snow.

- Wolverines are fierce animals. They can even scare grizzly bears away and steal their food.

Fact file

Lives: Northern Europe, Asia, and North America

Habitat: Tundra and forests

Length: 25–40 inches

Weight: 25–35 pounds

Life span: 7–12 years

Diet: Carrion, eggs, rodents, rabbits, moose, elk, and fruit

To keep other animals away from their food, wolverines spray it with a smelly liquid and bury it for later.

 In winter, wolverines use snow like a refrigerator. They cover extra food with snow so it will stay fresh for several weeks.

Ring-tailed lemur

- Ring-tailed lemurs have been known to fight using smells. Rivals waft smells at each other using their tails.

- Lemurs are primates and are related to monkeys.

- Ring-tailed lemurs are found only on the island of Madagascar, off the coast of Africa.

- Ring-tailed lemurs have 13 alternating black and white rings on their tails. They hold their tails high so other lemurs can see them when they search for food.

- Lemurs are expert climbers, but they spend a lot of their time on the ground sifting through fallen leaves for food.

Lemurs also spend a lot of time grooming their own and each other's fur. In fact, they have six special lower teeth that act like a comb.

A lemur's front paws have fleshy pads that help them with their grip when they climb.

A mother ring-tailed lemur carries her baby in her mouth for a few weeks after birth until the baby is strong enough to hang from her belly or ride on her back.

Fact file

Lives: Madagascar

Habitat: Forests and bushland

Length: 40 inches, including tail

Weight: 5–7.5 pounds

Life span: 16–19 years

Diet: Fruits, leaves, sap, and flowers

Ibex

- Ibex live on steep mountainsides where few other animals can climb.

- The ibex's hoof is split into two halves that work like pincers to grip onto steep rocky ledges.

- A baby ibex, or kid, can run and jump just a few hours after it is born.

- Male ibex have huge curved horns; females also have horns, but they are much shorter.

- Male ibex have beards that they use to spread their scent.

- An ibex can jump more than six feet straight up.

- Ibex lick mountain rocks to get extra salt that is missing from their leafy food.

Fact file

Lives: Europe, Asia, and Africa
Habitat: Mountain pastures
Length: 2.5–5.5 feet
Weight: 85–220 pounds
Life span: 10–16 years
Diet: Grass and leaves

Leopard

Fact file

Lives: Africa and southern Asia
Habitat: Forest and grasslands
Length: 3–6 feet
Weight: 65–200 pounds
Life span: 12–17 years
Diet: Antelope and deer

Leopards can kill prey much larger and heavier than themselves. They can even drag their food up into trees so other predators can't get to it.

A leopard's ears are five times more sensitive than a human's.

Leopards can jump about ten feet into the air.

Leopards are the largest cats that can climb trees. They have a strong tail that helps them balance on branches.

Leopards can go for ten days without drinking water. They get a lot of the water they need from the food they eat.

A leopard's spotted coat makes it harder for other animals to see its full shape among shadows, trees, and long grass.

A leopard points its whiskers forward when it is stalking prey, and folds them back when sniffing the air to locate prey.

Leopards rarely roar. Instead, they communicate with deep, raspy barks.

Duck-billed platypus

- The platypus is born with a sharp spur on the heels of its rear feet, which is used in fighting. A male's spur produces venom. Females lose their spurs during their first year.

- The platypus is one of just two types of mammals that lay eggs instead of giving birth to live young.

- The platypus's unique bill has special nerve endings that can detect nearby prey.

- Platypus babies are born with teeth, but these soon fall out. Adults do not have teeth.

Fact file

Lives: Eastern Australia

Habitat: Lakes and streams

Length: 12–18 inches

Weight: 1–4 pounds

Life span: 12 years

Diet: Crustaceans, insects, snails, and fish

A platypus can stay submerged underwater for up to two minutes, skimming the gravel bottom for food.

A platypus's flat tail is used to store food and as a swimming aid.

A platypus closes its eyes underwater and relies on its sensitive bill to find its way around.

Striped hyena

- Unlike their relatives that are known for their giggles and cackles, striped hyenas are typically quiet.

- Striped hyenas have one of the strongest bites of any animal. They can crack through a bone with their teeth.

- They look like big dogs or small lions, but in fact hyenas are more closely related to mongooses.

- Striped hyenas can hunt for food, but most of the time they steal the kills of larger animals.

- When it is ready to fight, a hyena raises the hair around its neck. This makes it look bigger and tougher.

Fact file

Lives: Africa

Habitat: Grasslands, woodlands

Length: 3–5 feet

Weight: 50–120 pounds

Life span: 12 years

Diet: Antelopes and zebras

Striped hyenas are mainly solitary, or live in small groups where the female is in charge.

 Striped hyenas are territorial and mark their area with a scent gland located on their rear ends. Each striped hyena has a unique scent.

Bush baby

🐾 Although they're small, bush babies can jump up to six and a half feet high!

🐾 Bush babies sleep all day and come out at night to look for food.

🐾 Bush babies have very big eyes for seeing in the dark, and they use their huge ears to pick up the sounds of nearby insects.

🐾 A bush baby's second toe has a much longer fingernail called a "toilet claw." The toilet claw is used for grooming.

🐾 A bush baby has two tongues. A small lower tongue is used for licking its fur clean.

Another name for the bush baby is "galago."

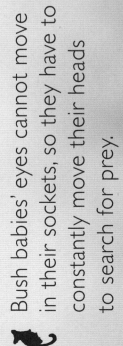 Bush babies' eyes cannot move in their sockets, so they have to constantly move their heads to search for prey.

Fact file

Lives: Africa

Habitat: Woodlands, savannas

Length: 8 inches

Weight: 5–10 ounces

Life span: 4 years

Diet: Insects, fruit, seeds, flowers, eggs, and tree gums

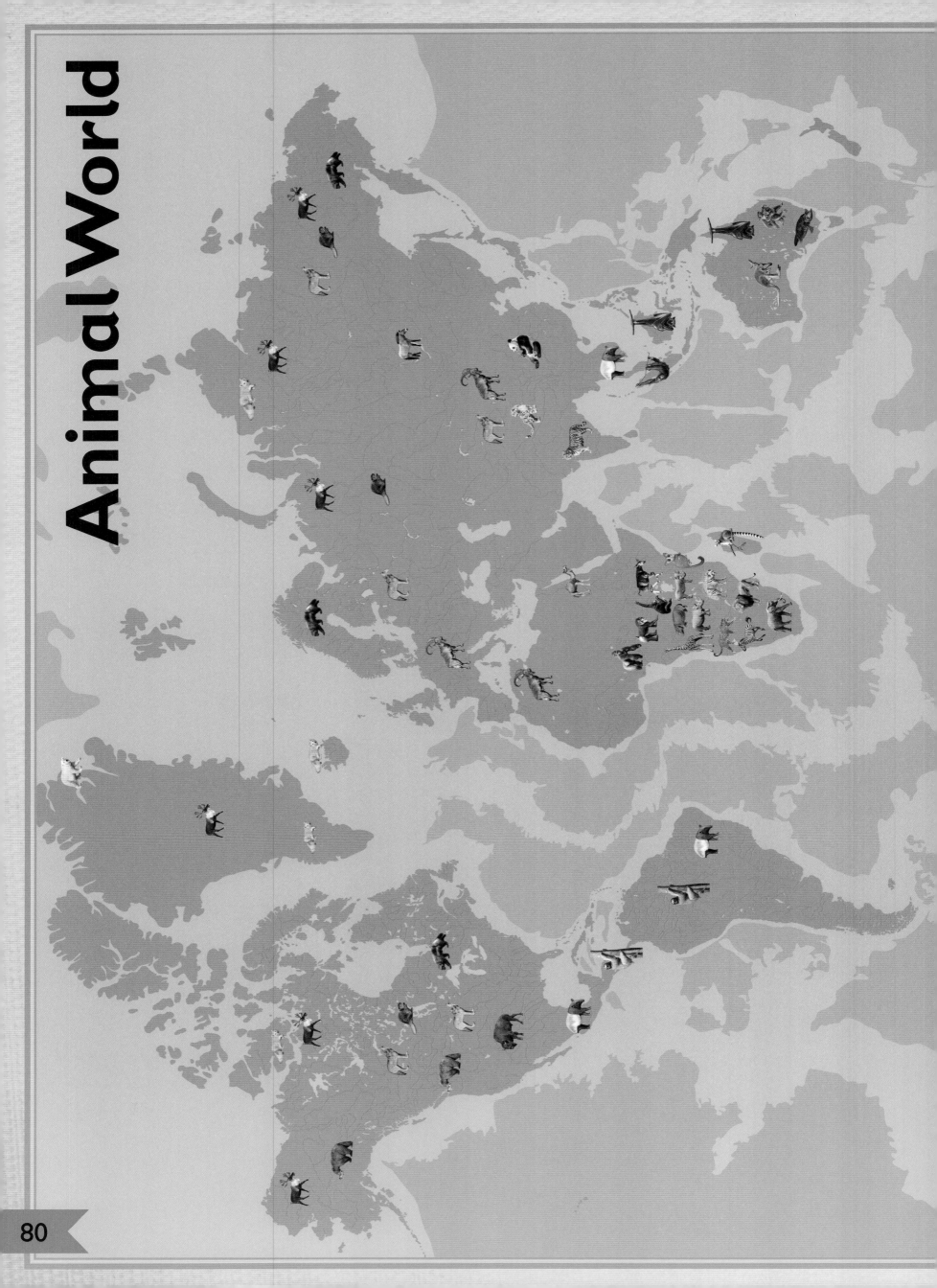